FROM THE HEART

D0770119

FROM THE HEART

MARILOU RENNIE, LCSW

To order additional copies of this book, contact:
Xlibris Corporation
1-888-795-4274
www.Xlibris.com
Orders@Xlibris.com
39790

CONTENTS

Dedicated to hospice patients and families everywhere.
Without them, there would be no stories.

ONE READER'S STATEMENT

These poems create a picture of the end of a human journey. Each ending is as unique as every life. The compassion, insightfulness and sometimes humor that is expressed in each poem is truly remarkable. This book has captured glimpses of the human condition and spirit at a difficult time. Marie Warner

ACKNOWLEDGEMENTS

This book would never have come to completion without the help from my family, friends and co-workers. Their continual support is what kept me going during this process. I wish to thank my family Bob, Mike, April and Mark Rennie for their unconditional support. I also could not have done this without the help of Beulah Warner who, along with my family, read and reread each page without complaint. In addition, I would like to thank my friend Judy Johnson. Her gentle insistence about hearing the story behind ever poem was invaluable. Because of her insightful persistance, a story accompanies every poem.

BOOKS

During my career as a Medical Social Worker, I have met many people. Everyone has a story to share. Each of us are unique and dependent upon each other to survive, so everyone's story is important. No matter how short or how long a story, all of our lives are intertwined. The stories that are in these pages are extraordinary tales about ordinary people like all of us.

BOOKS

Life.
An exclusive best selling novel
full of pages
yielding a wondrous narrative
only one unique individual
could ever detail.

Some books become sagas.
Chapters teeming with character
while others are short stories
with scarce pages to fill.

Some books are left
dormant on the shelf
full of blank pages.
Unfulfilled stories never
to be recounted.

Other books are
read and reread,
over and over.
Covers become faded,
pages curled at the corners,
binding cracked and worn.

A world full of books.
Each distinct
supporting each other.
Volumes to share
until
The End.

TOOTHPASTE

Nancy was a wonderful woman who was suffering from leukemia. She came onto hospice in June, one month before her eighty-second birthday, so she planned a birthday party for herself. She wanted it to be her memorial and so invited everyone she knew. Her plan was to die shortly after the party.

Nancy's disease progressed very slowly. Each time I visited her she would say, "I am sick and tired of being sick and tired." Nancy had been active her entire life and was very impatient with her dependence and the slow decline of her disease. She had moved in with her daughter and had fears that she would overstay her welcome. Her family was very close and devoted to her so the chance of that happening was nil.

Nancy had a wonderful outlook on life. She was very practical and felt it was her time to go. She wanted to just get on with it. In September she bought this large tube of toothpaste and said that it was would be the last tube. This poem is a result of the visit I did in early January after the Christmas holidays. Nancy died three months later. I was honored as the family printed this poem in her memorial.

TOOTHPASTE

She turned eighty-two last summer.
She knew she'd never see eighty-three
so she planned a final birthday party
inviting everyone she knew.

It would be her memorial.
Lots of hugs and goodbyes.
Then they could get on with their lives
and she would be ready to die.

Her disease is progressing slowly.
She's impatient with the pace.
She just wants it over,
"I bought my last tube of toothpaste."

Summer turns to Fall
as her toothpaste tube shrinks down.
Her patience is constantly challenged
as the disease dawdles on.

The tube is almost empty
as the Winter holidays roll around.
If you ask her about her Christmas
she'll disappointedly reply,
"I was given two more tubes of toothpaste."

BETWEEN HER LINES

This poem is about sixty-six year old Ronnie, who was diagnosed with terminal lung cancer two weeks prior to coming onto hospice. Ronnie was so matter of fact and sarcastic. Her sharp wit had everyone laughing. Her family gave it back just as quickly. Their caring could be over-shadowed by all the sarcasm, but the love did continue to shine through. Upon leaving after a visit one day, one of Ronnie's daughters walked me out to my car and told me that it helps the family so much that mom is still being herself.

This family reminded me so much of my own family. I immediately connected with their humor and saw the love that flowed along with it. I was able to give it back as easily as they gave it to me. It helped us connect immediately as they knew I understood the dynamics that had always helped them get through tough times.

When the family showed me the sweatshirt that Ronnie had made, I laughed so hard I had tears. I totally understood what Ronnie was trying to do. She was taking care of her family by telling them that she was not going to be around, but that she would be okay. Her wonderful humor was a comfort to us all.

Sarcasm can be used in such a healthy way if one teases another about strengths. That is what helped this family through their grief. Laughter can take the edge off the pain and reality of a difficult situation.

BETWEEN HER LINES

She's always been a straight shooter.
She says what's on her mind.
She displays her love through humor.
Her family knows how to read
between her lines.

Her recent terminal discovery
took her family by shock and surprise.
She takes it all in stride though,
using humor to get her by.

She's sarcastic with a quick wit.
Her family is glad that she's that way.
It's the mom with whom they've always known.
They lovingly give it back
from whence it came.

The family expresses comfort
after seeing what she had made.
"Goodbye Already" embossed on a sweatshirt.
They knew then that she'd be fine.
They'll always be able to read
        between her lines.

CROOKED SMILE

I had been following Linda, a forty-eight year old who was dying of a brain tumor, for about a year. My first impression was how happy she was even in the midst of dying. She was from a large family who were totally supportive and there for her.

From the moment Linda was told she was terminal, she embraced each day to the fullest. She had taken a lot of trips with her family and stated that her diagnosis was what gave her the opportunity to do just whatever she wanted to do.

Linda's decline was fast. She was sleeping most of the time and had stopped eating. It appeared that she had about one to two weeks left to live. A few weeks prior, Linda shared that she would not want to live if she couldn't speak. Now she was having difficulty finding words.

During my last visit to the home, I was standing next to Linda's bed with three of her family members. We were talking in low, hushed voices so we wouldn't disturb Linda while she slept. All of a sudden, there she was, smiling her crooked smile. Her eyes didn't open and it seemed like she was still asleep, but I believe Linda was listening and enjoying our conversation.

One's personality doesn't change because they are dying. They will cope with dying as they have coped with any other stressor that they have experienced in their life. People use the same coping skills that have always worked for them.

CROOKED SMILE

She's lived her life to the fullest.
She's embraced each of those days.
No matter what life has handed her,
she'll always display that crooked smile.

Her smile lights up a room
giving delight to those standing around.
She'll laugh at just about anything,
even when life jiggles her world.

She does have concerns about her sons.
How will they manage when she is gone?
Worry seldom hangs around long
as it's easily replaced
by that crooked smile.

She sleeps most of her days now.
The disease is gaining ground.
Family whispers nearby in soft, quiet voices
not wanting to make much noise.

Then
from out of nowhere,
when all her chips seem down,
she'll suddenly display
         her amazing,
sweet, crooked smile.

GAINING CONTROL

John, seventy-three, suffered a stroke six years prior, leaving him wheelchair bound and dependent with all of his needs. Three weeks before, John stopped eating and interacting with his family. He became weak and spent most of his days in bed. The doctors say that he is able to eat, he just refuses.

John understands and is aware, but unable to communicate except by nodding his head yes or no when asked a direct question. When I asked John if he wanted to die, a single tear appeared. His wife, Trudy, said that he was such a sociable and outgoing person before the stroke.

We all like to have control over our lives. John had so much taken away from him when he suffered the stroke. He found something though, he still could control. He could control whether he ate or not. People get tired of fighting an uphill battle knowing that it will never get any better. John was ready to go. John died peacefully one week later.

GAINING CONTROL

Sadness permeates his world.
Depression occupies his day.
Memories of a vital past,
mourning future lost.

Monotony invades his idle hours.
Dependent for six years.
Nodding once for "yes" or "no"
is all that he can do.

He's stopped eating to regain control.
His condition's becoming weaker.
When asked if he is ready to die,
a single tear appears.

He'll leave a legacy of sadness,
memories of depressed years.
After all that he has lost,
that's all he's left to give.

GOODBYE

Ed, sixty-four, suffered from cardiac disease for years. Ed and his wife, Mary, were told recently by Ed's physician that he could die at any time due to the extensive damage to his heart. Ed and Mary attempted to keep a normal routine in their life while cherishing each of those moments.

Quite often, when someone has suffered from a disease for years, it becomes routine as they go about their life. They may have suffered some setbacks, but have always bounced back. In the back of their mind, they know they could die at any minute, but always think there is time because with each setback, they recover and are back living their life again. When the actual event occurs, it still can be a shock to those involved, no matter how long the disease process has been.

GOODBYE

They knew his days were numbered.
They knew it wouldn't be long.
Still they thought they had time
before he would say
    goodbye.

Life went on as usual
even though they never forgot.
Aware that it could be soon
when he would say
    goodbye.

It happened quite suddenly
when he collapsed upon the floor.
As she rushed to his side she knew
that it was time for him to say
    goodbye.

She quickly knelt down beside him
holding onto each of his hands.
Their eyes locked giving comfort
as she quietly whispered
    Goodbye.

HEAVEN

This poem is a love story about eighty-eight year old Stanley. Stanley was dying from prostate cancer. He always spoke so lovingly of his wife Helen. She died recently after a lengthy illness. They had been married for over sixty-two years. Stanley had been Helen's caregiver for many years. In order to keep her strength up, he assisted Helen with exercises. To get her to stand up from a chair to keep her muscles limber, Stanley would motivate her by promising to give her a kiss if she stood up. So Helen would stand and he would then kiss her.

I asked Stanley one day about what his heaven would look like. He said that it will be a lot like our earth only there will be only goodness. Stanley said Helen loved shooting stars and he is convinced that she is one. Stanley's heaven will definitely have shooting stars.

HEAVEN

He's been thinking more about heaven
ever since his wife's been gone.
When it's his time, he'll gladly leave
to again
       be by her side.

He's been thinking more about what it's like,
although convinced of several truths:
There will be no more darkness, only light.
       No more evil, only good;
              no more illness, only health.

He knows she's up there waiting
in the image of a shooting star.
Flying free after years of illness.
Soaring through the cosmos
waiting for him to come.

He knows his time is near.
He's ready to let go.
When he crosses over
he'll grab for her shooting star.
He'll hang on tight and never let go,
to again
       be by her side
              forevermore.

ADDICTION

Many hospice patients suffer from lung cancer. Once their health has deteriorated enough to bring them onto hospice, smoking may be one of the few pleasures that they have left. Many of these patients are on oxygen twenty-four hours a day. Hospice cannot stress enough the dangers of smoking and oxygen use. I have experienced many patients that take off their oxygen and go outside to grab a cigarette, even though their breathing becomes labored. The addiction is that strong.

ADDICTION

One puff then two.
Pink lungs introduced to toxin.
The craving begins.

One cigarette leads to another.
The numbers gradually increase.
Lungs start to taint.
Open another cellophane pack.

Coughing spells,
hard to catch a breath.
Sit down for a smoke;
or maybe two.

A spot on the lung.
Chemotherapy, radiation.
Blackened lungs, terminal.
Oxygen tank now a constant pal.

One puff then two.

MEMORIES

Ruth, eighty-nine, suffered from Alzheimer's Disease. Cal, Ruth's husband and caregiver, was devoted to her. He helped her with all of her daily needs. Ruth always loved to dance and had been very active in their mobile home park community. Cal said that Ruth was always so detailed and meticulous in everything she did.

Ruth was astute enough at times to know that she could not remember. She must have felt trapped. I was told once by a physician, that an Alzheimer patient's brain is like swiss cheese. There are some holes where no memory can be retrieved right next to retrievable awareness.

MEMORIES

Her home is full of memories.
Sepia photos of relatives
taken generations ago.
Each frame individually selected,
prominently displayed with her gentle care.

An eighty-six pound marlin
hangs conspicuously on the living room wall,
surrounded by black and white photos
detailing that remarkable day.
     Her catch.

Memories exhibited throughout the home
reflect their life together.
Each clearly expressing
     her precise manner
          her painstaking care,
               her participation in life.

Now she just sits in her recliner,
struggling to organize all the stimuli
that surrounds her.
As her brain fills with jumbled thoughts,
she tearfully states,
     "I just can't remember."

MARILOU RENNIE, LCSW

MY ANGEL

This poem is about an elderly couple, Melvin and Grace, who had been married fifty-six years. Melvin suffered from dementia and cancer. Grace said that he had not eaten or spoken for five days. She knew his time was near.

Years ago, Grace tried to talk with Melvin about making funeral arrangements and he always refused to talk about it. Even with his diagnosis and decline, Melvin remained strong in his determination not to talk about his wishes or even his spiritual beliefs. As Melvin lay dying, his last words to Grace gave her comfort in knowing he believed in heaven after all.

Patients can let go when they know their loved ones will be OK. It is just the same with the loved ones. Families can let go as well when they know the patient will be OK.

MY ANGEL

He's never wanted to talk about dying,
about his wishes or make any plans.
She's had to carry that burden alone
hoping that one day he'd change his mind.

He's never wanted to talk about God,
about his beliefs or the afterlife.
She'd like to do this the way he wants
but she's running out of time.

She would like to know what he's thinking
as now she has to make those plans.
He is confused and no longer talking.
She'll have to handle this alone.

She went to say goodbye to him
giving him permission to leave.
She told him that she would be alright
because he'd be her angel up there.

He didn't respond at all.
She wasn't quite sure if he heard,
but the next day he said quite loud and clear,
"I'm ready to go now.
I'll be your angel up there."

FINAL GAME

Dick, fifty-one, had been angry most of his life. Anger was the only way he knew how to cope. He was divorced and had a fourteen year old son who lived with his mother in another state. Dick didn't see his son much at all due to the geographic distance.

When Dick was diagnosed with rectal cancer, he reacted with anger. During the course of his disease, he did mellow and become less angry. Toward the end of his life, when he knew his time was near, he had fears that he had burnt many bridges throughout his life. He was able to express his fears and concerns to me without anger.

About a week before Dick died, I met with him to talk about his son who was coming to visit in a few days. I asked him about his legacy and what did he want to leave behind for his son. He said that he wanted his son to know that he was a great kid and to remember all of the lessons that his dad taught him. Dick found peace days before he died.

I have had a few patients who struggle up until the end of their life and never find peace or resolution. Quite often it is someone who has had many regrets or who cannot come to terms with dying as they feel cheated out of life. They typically are not sure about life after death and are afraid that the things they had done wrong in their life, may impact their own dying process. It is always a wonderful thing to witness someone, like Dick, who are able to find peace by processing their life and find meaning.

FINAL GAME

He's played hard all of his life.
He's tackled and has come up bruised.
He'd angrily walk to the sidelines
when he didn't make a score.

Now he's in his final game.
Only a few more yards to go.
He's trying to play by the official rules.
He's not done that before.

He's never been a team player.
He's always survived alone.
Now with the clock ticking down,
the final minutes loom near.

He'll play his final scrimmage
trying hard not to fumble the ball.
With focused eyes on the goal line,
somehow I know he'll score.

ANGER

Robert came onto hospice suffering from terminal lung cancer. His lungs were damaged from a lifelong smoking habit. He lived with his wife and two teenage children. His nineteen year old son, Josh, had a difficult time controlling his anger toward his father. Each time his father lit up a cigarette, it would fuel Josh's anger. Josh felt that his dad was killing himself. He thought that if his father would stop smoking, he would be cured.

I met with Josh alone one day. We talked about anger and strategies for coping. He was interested in journaling to help express his feelings. I asked Josh to get some paper and just write down one sentence about how he was feeling. He wrote an entire page with the words, "I hate you, I hate you, I hate you!" He said that he felt better after writing things down.

A short while later, his father came into the room and lit up a cigarette. Josh yelled at his father, "I hate you!" Josh was shaking. I feared that he would punch a wall or someone. His mother said that Josh had always been an angry child.

ANGER

He is so angry at his father.
He is ready to explode.
His whole body shakes
with strong feelings trapped inside.

He cannot find the words.
He doesn't know what to say
so he screams "I hate you!" to his father.
Then stays angry all the more.

His dad has smoked for years.
He says it gives him joy.
He's never going to stop
though his lungs are giving out.

He wants his dad to stop
thinking maybe he will live.
But they both know it's too late,
so each cigarette fuels him more.

He'll stay angry at his father.
He'll scream at him some more.
He'll cry hard when it is over
carrying angry words
      for far too many years.

ONE MORE YEAR

I attended the funeral for Colleen, a sixty-four year old patient, who had been on hospice for almost two years. Colleen had suffered from breast cancer for ten years. Colleen and her family had an undying faith in God. She always believed that if she prayed enough to God, He would let her live.

Thirteen months before Colleen died, she had a vision of God while sitting in her family room. God asked her what she needed and she asked Him for one more year. Colleen wanted the year in order to travel and spend more time with her family.

During that thirteen months, Colleen was able to travel to the Midwest to visit with her siblings. She also had the time to spend with her husband, children and grandchildren. Colleen was such a strong, independent person and had a hard time letting go because she worried about her family. Her family said that the year gave them time to say goodbye and now they feel Colleen is at peace.

ONE MORE YEAR

She had a strong faith in God.
She believed with all her might.
She knew He would always be there
helping her through this life.

She fought her disease for years.
Things got a little tentative at times,
but she always would bounce back.
She knew it was because of God.

She outlived all their predictions.
She just wasn't ready to die.
There were too many things she wanted to do
and somehow not enough time.

She was sitting in her room one day
when suddenly He was there.
He asked her what she needed
and she said, "One more year."

Some prayers are indeed answered.
Some faith will always remain strong.
She always believed He would answer her prayer.
Now we know too
because He gave her
        one more year.

SHE

This poem was inspired by sixty year old Jennifer, who was dying of uterine cancer. Jennifer did not believe in any afterlife and had no fears about dying. Her life was full of zest and joy. Her upbeat personality drew many people to her. She handled dying like she handled any other challenge in her life. She was a perfect example of how one's personality doesn't change when one is dying. We all learn early in life how to cope and it quite often sustains us throughout our entire lifetime.

SHE

She laughs
She jokes
She teases
She loves.

She's appreciative
She's sensitive
She cares
She's upbeat
She's thoughtful.

She smiles
She's earnest
She's optimistic
She's passionate
She's dying.

She knows.

A TISSUE

Sandy shared this story at her mother's funeral. Her mother Liz, sixty-seven, had been ill for less than a month. Sandy said that it was comforting to find a tissue in her own shoe on the morning of her mother's funeral.

People feel comfort when seeing signs of a loved one. They believe that it is evidence that their loved one is OK. I have heard stories about lights being turned on or doors being unlocked. One example of this involves an elderly couple who lived in a retirement community. Right outside their bedroom window was a bright street light. The husband complained multiple times to the home owners association to replace the bright light with a lower wattage bulb to no avail. Hours after he died, the street light turned off and stayed off until after his funeral when it again burned brightly. His widow believes it was her husband's doing and said that it gave her peace to know that he is OK.

A TISSUE

She always had a tissue handy.
A tissue in the pocket
of every dress,
    every skirt,
        every jacket.

She wouldn't be caught without one.
A tissue was always nearby
to use at a moment's notice
on any day,
    any week,
        any time.

Going through her mother's clothes
on the eve of her expected death.
Sorting for the Goodwill bin.
Discarding the tissue found in the pocket
of every dress,
    every skirt,
        every jacket.

Getting dressed for the funeral,
she believes she received a sign
that her mother was alright.
She discovered something
inside her shoe
    blocking her foot,
        hidden from view.

A tissue.

TELL ME

I was asked by Kathy, a forty year old patient, "How do I die?" Kathy was a person who was totally in charge of every aspect of her life. She had pre-planned her funeral and was redecorating her home so that her husband would have a comfortable place to live after she was gone. She had a very strong religious belief which gave her comfort. She did not have a fear of dying. She just wanted to be in charge of it.

I told her that she would die her way. I shared that when she was ready to let go, it would happen. There is no right or wrong way to do this. It will happen when it was suppose to happen. She had a hard time grasping that concept as it was not tangible enough for her.

Kathy was suffering at the end of her life and was very tired and weary. She did die a few weeks after our conversation, which was not soon enough for her.

We all want to control our own lives. I can only imagine that it must be hard to let go as most of us spend our life doing the exact opposite. When given enough time though, most people do willingly let go when the time is right for them to do so.

TELL ME

Tell me how to die.
Tell me what to do.
I'm tired of this pain.
I'm trying to let go.

Tell me what comes next.
I really need to know.
I want to get this right.
Please tell me what to do.

She didn't understand.
She thought it would be clear.
Just follow your chosen path.
You'll know when to go.

When the time is right,
things will move along.
You're the driving force.
You'll know to let go.

Just tell me how to die.
Please tell me what to do.

THE CRACK IN THE DOOR

This poem is about the grieving process that one experiences after a loss. Quite often an anniversary date, a birthday or a song on the radio can trigger forgotten feelings once thought to be over. I wrote this poem on the four year anniversary of a friend's death. Kate died from breast cancer in 1997, two months after Princess Diana's death. I heard the song "Candle in the Wind" by Elton John, on the radio. It triggered immense feelings of sadness in me. I associated that particular song with Princess Di and Kate's death as the two deaths happened around the same time.

I was surprised by my feelings as I hadn't felt that way for quite a while. I have always hated the word "closure" when it is associated with grief. I don't believe there is ever closure as one never forgets their loved one. Time does heal and the immense pain does come to an end, but there is never closure. Even now, ten years later, I still think of Kate. Now, though, when I think of her, I have a smile.

THE CRACK IN THE DOOR

Sadness sneaked a peek
through the crack in the door.
A quick glance that suddenly
opened an old wound
leaving a familiar bruise.

Once a well known companion;
now most days forgotten.
The sudden appearance
brings up instant reminders
of the painful past,
like it was only yesterday.

Taken back in time,
the anniversary date
unlocks the door
engulfing the vulnerable soul.

Never to be forgotten,
the portal stays mostly sealed,
although it can be opened
at a moment's notice
allowing sadness access again
through the crack in the door.

A LADY

Sonia, a charming eighty-nine year old, suffered from lung cancer and was slowly declining. She reminded me of Loretta Young when Loretta would gracefully twirl into the room at the beginning of her weekly 1950's TV show.

Sonia was always thinking of others and continually doing thoughtful deeds. She had such dignity and grace. Sonia's husband was a lobbyist for the Republican Party in Sacramento and her life consisted of hosting many dignitaries in her home. Even when dying, Sonia carried herself with such beauty and sophistication.

A LADY

She's from a bygone era
where proper manners and grace were the norm.
Where women were the quiet
behind-the-scenes strength
which ultimately propelled the power.

The days when roles were strictly defined.
Etiquette was proper and held in high regard;
ethics and values were unwavering and true.
Where everyone honored the Golden Rule.

She has lived through a myriad of changes.
An evolving constant in her life.
A slow demolition of her beliefs;
a vaporizing of her role.

Even now, in the twenty-first century,
she continues to hold on
to what she has always believed in.
What defines who she is;
      grace,
           dignity,
                 a lady.

A classy lady indeed.

NATURAL SCIENCE

This poem reflects the beliefs of an eighty-two year old gentleman named George, who had been on hospice for over six months. Eighteen months before, his physician told him that he had six months to live. George was annoyed that he had lived that additional year.

George would talk science and mathematics freely as he could intellectualize those topics. He would never speak of any personal feelings about life, although he did share numerous stories about his career as an engineer. He avoided any discussion about what he was experiencing emotionally.

Toward the end of his life, when his decline was obvious, George requested palliative sedation. Palliative sedaton is used to control pain at the end of one's life. It is rarely used. Patients are sedated in order for them to have relief from uncontrolled physical pain. George's pain was controlled, but his emotional pain was great. He was not a candidate for this procedure.

George was convinced that his doctor would approve the procedure and that the procedure would take place in a few days. He was calm and relaxed about it all. He believed that death was a natural event. George died a few weeks later without the palliative sedation procedure.

NATURAL SCIENCE

He has a scientific mind.
He was an engineer by trade.
Facts, information, equations.
He just fit right in.

He believes that life involves three steps;
birth, maturity then death.
It is just the way things are.
No point, no reason, no rationale.

After eighty two years of living
he's concluded his life had no purpose.
It's all a scientific conclusion.
Breathing in and breathing out.
It is the natural order of things.

He will likely die within a week.
His cancer has spread throughout.
He'll be sedated and sleep til the end.
That's how he wants to go.

He is somber but ready these last few days.
He is not afraid at all.
But somehow this appears so unnatural,
but to him
          it is the most
                    natural thing of all.

THE PROTECTOR

Seventy-nine year old Frank suffered from end-stage Alzheimer's. He was married fifty-four years to Agnes, who now cared for him. Frank was taken to the Emergency Room one night because he went after Agnes with a kitchen knife. Agnes, appropriately, feared for her safety.

In a moment of clarity, Frank was able to speak of the concerns he had for Agnes's safety. Frank appeared to understand every now and then, but just couldn't quite grasp things. Even though his words made no sense, his concern about Agnes was obvious.

Agnes agreed that the optimal plan was for Frank to go to a nursing home. Frank said that he would go if that would keep Agnes safe.

THE PROTECTOR

He fears for her safety.
He knows she is at risk.
He's been her protector
for over fifty years.
He can't stop being that
    just yet.

You can tell he is intelligent
by the way he phrases his words.
Articulating eloquent concerns for his wife,
he'll always do what he needs to do.

Last night he saw a stranger in his home.
He went after the intruder with a kitchen knife.
His primary focus was to protect his wife,
but Alzheimer's had turned the tables on him.

Somewhere deep inside he knows.
Occasional moments of clarity do surge.
He's aware his wife needs protection,
so he'll willingly move to where they say,
as the protection she needs
    is from him.

HER DAD

Fifty-nine year old, Sandy, was on hospice for only one week. When I met with Sandy's husband, Jim, he shared that his step-daughter Jennie, was like a daughter to him. He helped raise her since she was eight years old. Jim wanted to adopt Jennie from the beginning, but Jennie would always say no as she had hopes that her father would return and the two of them would then have a perfect father/daughter relationship.

During the course of this initial visit, Jim shared that Jennie feared that she would have no family once her mother died. Jennie was afraid that she would lose contact with her step-dad. I suggested to Jim that he tell Jennie that he would still like to adopt her. I wasn't sure that one could adopt an adult, but I said the ritual of the process would be just as strong as a legal one.

Jim really liked that idea, and a few weeks after Sandy died, he did ask Jennie again about adoption. She was receptive to the idea and felt it was wonderful. They both checked into the process and learned that one could be adopted as an adult. Jim and Jennie have been father/daughter emotionally for years, now it would become legal.

HER DAD

He's raised her since she was eight.
He wanted to adopt her back then.
But she always said no when asked
as she hoped one day,
her father would return.

The two have a loving relationship,
just like a dad and his daughter should have,
but she never let go of the dream
that someday her father would come.

She still feels abandoned by him
even though it's been almost thirty years.
She can't quite see the love
of the one who raised her.
She won't let go of that futile dream.

Now that her mother lay dying,
her fears of abandonment remain strong.
She's afraid she'll have no family at all
once her mother is gone.

But he did ask her one more time.
She has been a daughter to him.
This time she said yes.
She now knows who her father really is;
      her dad.

QUIETLY

One's personality doesn't change during the dying process. The coping skills they used throughout life, are once again used. It is what one is comfortable with and it is the same coping skills that had worked for them in the past.

When I spoke with the husband of this patient, he expressed comfort in that she died quietly. The way she died did not surprise him at all. It was how he knew her to be and it gave him peace.

QUIETLY

She required his help
so he spent most of his day
caring for her needs.
Few visitors stopped by.
They rarely left the house.
Their days slowly passed,
     quietly.

They've been married for years.
The children live away.
They spent most days alone,
he attending to her,
patiently, without complaint,
     quietly.

Her illness took an abrupt turn.
The end came quite suddenly,
but he felt comfort in knowing
that she died the way they lived,
     quietly.

THE SECRET

Jackson, fifty-eight, was brought to the Emergency Room by his wife, Joan. Joan had noticed Jackson becoming confused and wobbly on his feet. Later it was revealed that Jackson was told six weeks before that he had lung cancer which had spread to his brain. He chose, at that time, not to tell anyone. The Emergency Room physician thought that Joan was aware of Jackson's cancer. When the doctor mentioned it to Joan, she was shocked.

Jackson was admitted to hospice at that time. Joan took a leave of absence from her work to care for her husband. Jackson continued his attempt to cover up that anything was wrong, even though he became more and more confused. At the end of his life, he was in a place that was not scary for him as he didn't understand what was happening to him.

Denial is a very powerful coping mechanism. Jackson could not face dying and so it was safer for him to deny that anything was wrong. Intellectually he knew the truth, but he could not emotionally face the reality of what was happening to him.

THE SECRET

He's kept silent for six weeks.
He's hidden it all inside.
He didn't want anyone to know;
    especially himself.

His family started to notice symptoms.
Signs he tried to disguise.
The doctors mistakenly let his secret out.
Cancer suddenly revealed.

He has moment of foresight,
trying to grasp each day anew.
But confusion has a stronger pull
permitting protection from the truth.
Keeping the secret safe
    from him.

SHE LEFT US

We often have patients that are on the hospice program for one to two years. It becomes routine to drive over to their part of town and turn down their street. After the death, one can feel the loss of not turning down that street any more.

This poem is about such a case. I had been following Marie, sixty-eight, for over eighteen months. She was diagnosed with lung cancer and had outlived her doctor's prediction by a year. She was cared for by Will, her son's friend, who himself suffered from cancer. Initially Marie had accepted Will into her home to care for him. When she became ill, their roles were reversed as Will then became her caregiver. Later Marie's son came to assist and be the primary caregiver as her needs became too much for Will.

Marie was one of the most loving, caring and delightful souls I have known. She utilized the hospice team so perfectly. She had many friends and a huge family. Everyone loved her as she was so loveable. She dealt with her disease with grace and dignity. Her decline was swift. She touched many hearts, including the hospice staff.

I woke from my sleep one night thinking about her. The first time it was a little after 1AM and then again at 2:15AM. When I awoke at 2:15AM, I looked up to the ceiling and said to myself, "Marie if you are here, have a wonderful journey." I found out the next day that she was pronounced dead at 2:30AM by a hospice nurse. I would like to think she stopped in to say goodbye.

SHE LEFT US

She left us with her essence.
A tender spirit embracing our hearts.
A gentle nature pulling us in
welcoming us into her world.

She left us with her sweetness.
A piece of candy always nearby;
a chocolate chip cookie within arm's reach;
a big bear hug before we'd depart.

She left us with her thoughtfulness.
Sharing her life while caring about ours.
Always thinking of others.
Always knowing their needs.
Not able to let go
until the moment she knew
we would be fine.

She left us with many riches.
Memories of a wondrous soul.
But the hardest part of all is
        She left us.

HIS LAST BREATH

I went out to do my initial social work visit with Fred, eighty-eight, and his family. Fred had only been on hospice for one day. He was unconscious when I arrived and so I spent most of my time with his wife, Vera. I explained hospice services and the grieving process to Vera. Vera was stressed over what to do at the moment Fred died. Even after I explained how to contact hospice, she still had some anxiety about it all.

I know that patients leave this earth on their own terms. Often I have seen patients wait for a special date, a special phone call or visitor. They also wait until they know that their loved one is going to be okay. I believe that Fred had a sense that a hospice worker was in the home and would be available to assist the family at his death. I also believe it gave Fred's family a sense of peace having me there to make the call to hospice for them.

We all have control over when we leave this earth. I frequently witness patients waiting for a birthday, an anniversary or some unfinished business that is important for them to complete. I remember a patient who was unconscious and had not had anything to eat for almost three weeks. I visited weekly toward the end of his life. During the final two visits that I made to his home, he was in a deep sleep and not responsive. I went out on a Thursday to make a visit and found him sitting up and alert in his hospital bed. He told me that he wasn't going to die today. I asked him, "Why is that?" He replied, "Because tomorrow is my birthday." As I was leaving, I prepared his wife for a decline over the weekend. He died four days later. Patients let go when the time is right for them.

HIS LAST BREATH

They knew his time was close.
He'd been unconscious for three days.
With respirations slowing down,
he paused between each breath.

They didn't quite know
what they needed to do,
who they were suppose to call,
when he took that final breath.

They were appreciative
when I showed up at the door
explaining what they had to do,
who they had to call,
when it was his time to go.

They were still a bit nervous
wondering if this would all work out,
when his daughter came to me and said,
"He took his final breath."

We walked into his room
to see if it were true.
Standing there, we watched his chest rise
one more time,
      witnessing
            his last breath.

They were relieved to know
that he finally was at peace.
Thankful that I was there
to call who had to be called,
to do what had to be done,
after he took
      his last breath.

TO FIND THE WORDS

Working in this field, one has a clear understanding of what it is like to work with families in grief and crisis. All of us have suffered losses in our lives along the way, but the depth of the pain we felt eases up over time.

Our caring and compassion comes from the understanding of the deep pain that our patients and families struggle with. In order to come back the next day to do it all over again, we cannot experience the deep pain that they currently feel.

But then, our lives continue on as well. We can suffer losses and grief while working with others struggling with the same emotions. I sent this poem in a card to a close friend after learning of the death of her nineteen year old granddaughter, Jessi. Jessi was a passenger in a car that was hit head-on by a drunken driver. Jessi was in her first year of college and was blossoming into a fine, young woman working toward her lifelong goal of becoming a school teacher.

TO FIND THE WORDS

It's so hard to find the words
to express exactly how I feel.
If I say, "My heart aches for you,"
then it sounds more about me,
    than about you.

I can't even imagine how you feel,
so where do I really start?
Does, "I'm so sorry" really help?
Familiar words that may miss their mark.

I want to capture your soul.
To surround you with total love.
To protect you from your pain,
but how do I tell you so?

Maybe there are no words.
No language to express.
But then I guess you already know,
I am always here for you
    no matter what.

SHE LOVES HIM

Seventy-two year old George was divorced from his wife, Gloria, for seven years. Although they no longer were married, they remained close friends. Gloria had moved to another state taking Samantha, the family cat, with her. Georges's decline was quick. I called Gloria to inform her that George was actively dying. She asked me to tell George that she loves him.

I went into George's room and softly whispered into his ear as she requested. His eyes were open, but he wasn't able to speak. About three hours later, George died. I called Gloria to inform her of George's death. She said that she already knew as Samantha had started crying and wanted to be picked up. Gloria told me that George loved Samantha and she felt that the cat sensed his death. Gloria said that it gave her peace.

SHE LOVES HIM

She said to tell him
that she loves him.
A tender affirmation
powerfully condensed
into three simple words.

Bending softly near his side,
I whispered in his ear
like she asked me to.
Three final words
to send him on his way.

A thousand miles away,
her cat cried the moment he died,
pleading to be picked up.
She begged for attention,
meowing, weeping, pacing.

Somehow the cat sensed
the moment of his death.
She knew.
She loved him too.

MORE THAN WHOLE

Sixty-year old Ted was mentally challenged due to a brain infection when he was a small child. He met his wife, Linda, in special education classes in grammar school. He couldn't read or write and depended upon Linda. She was pretty stubborn, but with his happy disposition, they made a perfect balance.

Linda's sister, Sandy, lived nearby and assisted them as needed. Ted was diagnosed with melanoma several months before he died. Even though his decline was rapid, Ted always had a smile. His wife had some medical problems as well and was in a nursing home recovering from pneumonia during this time. Ted was able to visit her a few times each week.

The night before Ted died, it appeared that he had a massive bleed in his brain. He couldn't walk, his speech was garbled and he had trouble swallowing. Ted died the next afternoon. The family went to the nursing home to tell Linda of the news and stayed with her throughout the evening. The nursing home called Sandy at 5AM the next morning to tell her that Linda had died. Linda's death was unexpected, but the family had some peace knowing that Ted and Linda were together again.

MORE THAN WHOLE

They were both mentally challenged.
Their struggles drew them near.
Each had their own limitations,
but together they became
more than whole.

One relied on the other
to get them through each day.
With perseverance and will
they created a stable home.

He had a happy disposition.
Not much would get him down.
He easily produced a quick smile
because he knew
she made him whole.

They worried more about her
when the doctors told them the news.
How would she manage without him?
What would happen when he was gone?

He quietly slipped away one afternoon.
It was sudden and caught them off guard.
They comforted her the best they could,
but hours later, she too was gone.

They were meant to be together.
Now we know they always will.
Eternally side by side.
Together both are now
        more than whole.

MYRA

John, sixty-seven, had been on hospice for twenty-one months suffering from pancreatic cancer. John's prognosis was very grim, but he outlived every prediction. He had such a strong will to live.

John fell the night before he died. His wife, Christina, and brother Bill, put him back into bed. They called hospice to let them know what was going on. The hospice nurse said she would come right out. About thirty minutes later, the doorbell rang. As Bill got up to answer the door, the doorbell rang again. They assumed it was the night hospice nurse. When Bill opened the front door, there was no one there. Bill stated that he felt a large gust of wind blow in through the doorway.

The following morning, John's regular nurse and I went out to do a visit as it appeared that his death was imminent. We wanted to give support to the family. As we walked in, Myra, the family dog, came up and sniffed me. Myra was a brown and white mixed breed dog. When she walked, her little ears would stick straight up while her short, stubby tail would wag swiftly.

On each visit that I made, Myra would habitually sniff me and then go back to her bed. On this particular day, Myra would not leave my side the entire time I was in the home. She kept licking my hand and stayed right beside me. Several times I went out to the front porch to talk with Bill, as he had been sitting out there. Each time that I returned into the home, Myra was waiting for me right inside the front door.

MYRA

Myra's been a part of the household
since they brought her into their home.
She loves their companionship,
her big comfy bed,
but especially those doggie bones.

She likes to welcome all the guests
who walk through their front door.
She'll check them out,
a quick sniff or two
then back to her bed on the floor.

Did she hear the doorbell ring
when there was no one at the door?
Did she sense his spirit leaving
when the gust of wind blew hard?

I guess we'll never know,
but I have a hunch she was aware,
as she wouldn't leave my side today
while her master slowly died.

Dogs have a keen intuition
and a strong desire for love.
Time will heal the pain for the family.
I hope it's the same for dogs.

THE TEACHER

Marty, aged forty-nine, grew up tough. He had to be tough as his parents struggled with addictions when he was a child. There was never enough money or time available to nourish him as he grew. Even though Marty's life wasn't easy, he was a hard worker and never gave up.

I met Marty soon after he was diagnosed with terminal cancer. At first he dealt with things the only way he knew how, fighting and grappling with what life had dealt him. In time, I saw Marty soften and come to terms with his condition. During that period, Marty was able to recognize the care and compassion given to him by others. Marty was able to respond in kind.

Marty had such grace and dignity during this process. It was a dramatic change for him, but one that slowly evolved over several months. In the end, Marty was able to find his peace. He taught us all that it is never to late to change.

THE TEACHER

He never was an excellent student.
He struggled with lessons each day.
But now that he has become the instructor,
his teachings are most profound.

He has become proficient
in the art of dying with poise.
Showing us style in the process,
showering us with grace.

It has been a dramatic transformation.
A tough lesson learned rather swift.
But he has been able to handle the burden
teaching us as he goes.

He will leave a legacy.
One he could never predict.
He is teaching us all
how it is never too late
to open our hearts,
    to change things around
        if only just given a chance.

THE OBITUARY

This poem is about Donna, a seventy-eight year old who was on hospice for over nine months. During that time, Donna constantly complained about her life and her current situation. She resisted any help or advice that I or anyone else offered. Donna just didn't want to change. She would not follow the advice of her doctor or the hospice nurse and as a result suffered unnecessary pain. I saw a bitter, unhappy woman on each visit, who was continually resistant to any comfort that could possibly improve the quality of her life.

Over the months that I knew her, I made many attempts to offer support. Donna always wanted to be in control and felt that her life was out of control. I tried to have her focus on those things which she did have control. I spoke of how she had control over how she handled her disease. Donna wouldn't buy any of it.

During my final visit to her home, I felt that I got a sneak peak into who she truly was. Donna grabbed my hands in a sweet gesture and teased me about something. It was at that moment that I saw a youthful, cheerful soul. Unfortunately it was only for a moment. Donna died a few days later. I pray that she found her peace.

Quite often patients are angry about dying. Given time, many do find peace and acceptance. It is not easy, but I believe the key is just letting go. It can be scary as none of us want to lose control over our life.

THE OBITUARY

The obituary in the newspaper
told the story of her life.
Highlighted by a black and white photo
showing a youthful, happy face.

It amazed me to read about her past
so full of zest and vitality.
Involved in wondrous activities;
accomplishments galore.

I read about a woman
who lived her life to the fullest;
who went after her dreams;
who participated in her world.

I only knew her to be a victim
this last year of her life.
Someone who was afraid to change.
Whose suffering seemed voluntary.
A punishment from God.

Her life spanned seventy-eight years
of which I knew her less than one.
The obituary told of happy times.
I pray she's happy now.

CONNECTED

Kathy, aged forty-two, died two months after a diagnosis of brain cancer. She left behind a husband and two teenagers. On the same day, Emily, eighty-one years old, died after struggling with lung cancer for five years. She was widowed and had three adult children and five grandchildren.

Each life appeared unrelated to the other. One was young; the other old. One was newly diagnosed; the other not. Somehow Kathy's death may seem a bit sadder because she left behind two teenagers. Teenage years should be about dances, movies and going out with friends, not about the loss of a parent. On the other hand, Emily also left behind family who loved her. The age of a person does not diminish the grief for anyone. Yes, Emily may have had a full and long life, but those left behind are grieving just as hard as Kathy's family and friends. The connection between both women is loss. The death of a loved one is difficult, no matter what led up to that loss.

CONNECTED

One was young,
the other old.
Somehow they connected.

One had teenagers,
the other's were grown.
Somehow they all connected.

One's illness was short,
the other's way long.
Somehow they still connected.

Two families in grief.
Two lives suddenly gone.
Yes, they definitely are connected.

THE RING

Following a death, one can be more prepared for those times that they know will be hard, such as a birthday or an anniversary date. When one knows that a particular day may be hard, they can gear themselves up to handle what that day may bring. It is the times that we don't see coming, that knock us over.

John's grief was still fresh and he hadn't had much time yet to process those feelings. John experienced unexpected grief when his wedding ring was cut off. The ring was a symbol of his marriage and the physical act of cutting the ring was a strong reminder of what he had just lost. His grief was suddenly magnified.

THE RING

He's had the ring for years.
He wears it all the time.
A special keepsake;
a commitment of his love.

She put the ring on his finger
so many years ago,
symbolizing a precious vow
to be always by his side.

He stumbled and took a fall.
ER corridors, x-rays, physicians
triggering memories
still fresh in his mind.

He injured his finger in the fall.
His hand is swollen and bruised.
The only solution was to cut off the ring
symbolizing his love
for the woman he lost
three days ago.

HER LITTLE BIRD

This poem is about Pamela, who had been married for thirty-five years to Jim. Jim had always taken care of her. Their roles were reversed seven months before when Jim was admitted to hospice care. Pamela had to step up and manage those things which Jim had always cared for in the past. She had many questions on how to manage during the course of his decline. She was doing a marvelous job, but didn't quite have the confidence to see it in herself. On one of my last visits to their home, Pamela shared the story about her little bird.

There is a unique relationship between families and the hospice staff. We are all strangers at the admission to hospice, but with each interaction and visit, something wonderful often happens. I feel honored to have patients and families welcome me into their home and share something as intimate as dying. As hospice workers, we allow them the opportunity to deal with what is happening to them in their unique, individual way. The connection goes both ways and it can be tempting to get involved more than one should. A hospice worker must always remember their professional boundaries. If one got too emotionally involved with a family, it could lead to burnout. It is important for the staff to be able to process these experiences in a way that is helpful to them. Many of my co-workers jog, garden, journal or some other activity that helps them release their own emotions in order for them to get up the next day to do it all over again.

HER LITTLE BIRD

She told me about her little bird.
How he sits quietly on her left shoulder.
No one else can see him,
but he is always there for her.

She just has to turn her head
to know he's sitting there,
waiting to hear what she has to say.
She shares her thoughts with him.

When she doesn't know where to turn.
When she doesn't know what to do,
she consults with her little bird.
It helps when she can talk it out.

She told me about her bird today.
How he listens as she talks.
She says her bird always has the answers
as her little bird
          is me.

TO MOVE ON

This poem reflects a conversation I had with Susan, a fifty-nine year old patient dying of cancer. She was very open about her dying and easily accepted her terminal diagnosis. Her biggest concern was her two adult sons. She kept telling them, "It's okay to move on." Her sons were rather quiet and didn't say much about what they were feeling or how they were doing. Susan had a sense of relief when they came to her and said, "It is okay to move on."

Some people need to talk, some don't. Some need to share, some don't. The important thing is for patients and families to communicate their needs and concerns with each other. Quite often one can assume what they think the other wants. Without asking them, miscommunication can occur. Susan and her sons spoke in such a way that both understood and heard the other. Because of that clear communication, Susan was able to let go of her worry about her sons.

TO MOVE ON

She knows her time is short.
Her life now near its end.
She worries about her sons.
She wants them to move on.

She raised them all alone.
They've always been a team.
She's told them more than once,
"It's okay to move on."

She knows it's hard on them
to watch her slow decline.
They don't say a lot,
but their love is all around.

She hoped they'd be alright
and now she knows they will
as they came to her and said,
"It's okay to move on."

UNSPEAKABLE PAIN

Ryan's grandpa had been sick for only a month and swiftly declined. Ryan, who was eight years old, was there when his grandpa died. Ryan had never experienced a death before and didn't quite know what to do, to think or to feel. These emotions were all new to him.

I met with Ryan in the living room as the family had asked me to speak with him. I saw him sitting so rigid as if he were afraid to move. He didn't quite know what to do. While I was offering support to him, he stared intently at me trying to figure things out. He never said a word, but when I started speaking of his Grandpa, a single tear appeared and flowed slowly down his right cheek. Ryan's tear spoke volumes.

Children grieve as hard as adults. They just don't have the vocabulary to express those feelings. Even with adults, it can often be just as difficult, as feelings can run the gamut from one moment to the next. One typically feels a multitude of feelings, not just one single emotion at a time.

UNSPEAKABLE PAIN

He sat there so silently.
His rigid back ramrod straight.
Not wanting to move.
Not wanting to break apart.

He looked so solemn
staring directly at me
without saying a word
while I offered comfort
to acknowledge his loss.

With trembling lips
he listened to my words
gulping to catch his breath.
With the mention of his grandpa's name
a single tear appeared
then slowly trickled
down his sad face.

SO HE IS

This poem is the story of Danny, a fifty-three year old patient who was on hospice for almost a year. Danny had an extensive history of alcohol and drug abuse. He had been in prison multiple times and had two felony convictions on his record. This poem was written the day he told me about his parents beating him as a child. Danny learned how to cope with anger early in life.

While Danny was in prison he suffered a heart attack. At that moment, he had an out-of-body experience. He spoke of meeting an angel. It was then that Danny turned his life around. Since that time, he has been clean and sober while helping other drug addicts and alcoholics.

Danny took full responsibility for the damage he had done to his heart by abusing drugs. He could not see the impact he made on others. What I saw was the gentle man Danny had become. Danny was continually hard on himself for his past indiscretions. I would always assure him that, because of his past, he was able to effectively help other addicts. He had the insight and understanding of their struggles that others did not.

SO HE IS

He was beaten as a child.
Bruises and scars abound.
He learned all about shouting and anger.
And so he was.

His parents said he was a burden.
He felt like a failure every day.
They said he would amount to nothing.
And so he did.

He hung out with a rough crowd.
He learned all about alcohol and drugs.
They called him an addict.
And so he was.

He ended up in prison
where a heart attack saved his life.
He knew he would have to change.
There would be no second chance.

It was then he turned his life around.
Helping others who were like him.
Giving courage to stay clean.
Motivation for a better life.
And so he does.

He cannot see the impact he makes.
Old labels are hard to renounce.
He still feels like a failure.
Everyone else sees a caring, gentle man.
And so he is.

TO LET GO

Rob, fifty-six, suffered from lung cancer. I had been meeting with him weekly for about three months. Rob was struggling with his dying. He had a sense of urgency about himself, always worrying that he wouldn't have time to do things the correct way.

Rob wasn't able to recognize the good he had done in his life. He had a successful career as a engineer until his illness forced him to retire. He loved cars and had rebuilt a 1965 red Corvette; his pride and joy. He spoke often about his two divorces, wishing that he had done things differently. In time, Rob was able to let go of some of his past. He started to focus on the moment and slowly accept who he was.

I learned from Rob that it is never too late to change. After much soul searching, Rob was able to find his peace.

TO LET GO

I've been telling you for weeks
to go when you needed to go.
Striving to give you the courage
to let go to find your peace.

You've suffered for so long.
You've been ready for a while
as I tried to impart some comfort
in your struggle to let go.

I wish I could have been there
to say goodbye that night,
but it was meant to be that way.
It was time for you to go.

I'll miss the talks we had.
In your dying you taught me about life.
It's time for me to say goodbye.
It's not easy to let go.

THE TRAIL

Ninety-five year old Ruth was fiercely independent with a spunky, delightful personality. She had been diagnosed with cancer several years prior, but still lived safely alone. Ruth's niece, Ann, was her only family and was devoted to her. Ann checked in on Ruth frequently.

Ruth was declining and it was clear she could no longer live alone without help in the home. I helped Ann arrange attendant care for her aunt. Ruth did not like this idea at all, but reluctantly agreed.

Before we finalized the arrangements, Ruth suffered a major stroke and died quite suddenly. Ann and I discussed how Ruth would have hated having attendant care in the home. Ann believed that Ruth chose the only way that was acceptable to her. It gave Ann peace knowing that Ruth died the way she lived; on her own terms.

THE TRAIL

She could see the end of the trail.
She didn't like what she saw.
She always knew her journey would end,
but was never ready to step off.

She would never acknowledge the impact
of her distance down that path,
though her shoes were showing some wear
and her back hunched from decades on the road.

She always did things her way.
She wasn't about to change now.
It was that spunky spirit that kept her going.
More than others she passed by.

She couldn't climb that final hill.
The path was much too steep.
She set her load down on the trail.
That's when she chose to go home.

"I'M YOUR DAUGHTER, LINDA"

Eighty-three year old, John, suffered from end state dementia. He had been residing in a Board and Care home for several years. His daughter Linda, visited on a regular basis. On each visit, she lost a little bit more of her father. But, only as a child can, she held onto the memories of who he used to be.

When a loved one suffers from dementia, families grieve way before the actual death. They lose their loved one slowly and so their grieving process may stretch over years. Linda may feel a sense of relief when her father actually dies. She has already lost the father of whom she knew and loved. At the death, quite often families feel that their loved one is now at peace and no longer suffering.

"I'M YOUR DAUGHTER, LINDA"

"I'm your daughter, Linda",
she whispered so soft, so sweet.
Bending down to meet his gaze,
overlooking the disease
that stole his mind away.

A stranger easily sees
the ravages of his affliction.
Hastily disregarding
the elementary, amnesic thinking
which complicates his world.

A daughter's love withstanding,
she holds onto all that remains.
One final, fragile connection,
a linkage to their former life,
"I'm your daughter,
     Linda".

FOR YOU

A family of four, pulling a travel trailer, were traveling along a steep downhill grade on a busy highway. They were from Oregon and were on summer vacation. The east/west highway is separated so that the westbound lanes are high above the eastbound lanes. I can only imagine that the driver miscalculated the sharp drop, picked up too much speed and lost control. The car and trailer went over the embankment rolling over and over until it stopped near the bottom close to the eastbound lanes.

I came upon the accident driving eastbound as the helicopter was landing to pick up the injured. Our lanes were closed temporarily in order for the helicopter to set down. I found out later that a twelve year old girl died at the scene. Witnessing the outcome of such a tragedy makes one pause.

FOR YOU

My job takes me all around the area,
quite often along the same route.
Frequently in my travels
I pass that same spot along the highway
and I always think of you.

I don't slow down my car
but I glance over at that embankment.
I pause and think of that day.
I offer a small prayer
and a moment of silence
      for you.

It had to have been so scary
when the car went over that cliff;
ejecting you from the back seat;
propelling you onto its path.
What was going through your mind
or did you have a chance to think at all?
I only pray you felt no pain.

I came upon the scene not long after.
The police had stopped all traffic
so the helicopter could come down
to rescue your parents and your brother too.
It was too late to save you.

But I just want you to know
that whenever I am driving
along that stretch of the road
I always pause and think of that day;
I offer a small prayer
and a moment of silence
      for you.

SEASHELL

Larry was a forty-six year old patient that I followed for almost a year. He had been in terrible pain for years suffering from a skin disease. His pain was constant; though he never complained. I so admired his strength and courage. He came onto hospice suffering from terminal lung cancer.

The last few months Larry was on hospice, I saw him almost weekly. He shared many stories of his life of which he wasn't proud. During the last year of his life he became very spiritual. He would talk about how God had impacted him and how he could now look at his life in an entirely different way.

During my last visit to his home, he shared that I had made a huge impact on him. He said that he felt a strong connection. I shared that I felt it also. He had a seashell collection and I asked him to show me a seashell from heaven so I would know that he was OK. He said that he would.

He died four days later on a Sunday afternoon. I was driving in my car when I suddenly thought of Larry. When I returned to work the next day, I found out he died at that same moment. I knew then he was OK.

Every now and then a patient will touch me more deeply than others. I have tried to understand why that is and cannot come up with any definitive answer. There is no common age or personality type that I am aware of. The situations have all been entirely different. Somehow a patient will touch me deep in my soul like no other. Larry was one of those special angels that walked into my life.

SEASHELL

Show me a seashell.
Put one in my path.
Make it sparkle
so I will see.
Show me that you're fine.

You had a difficult time
living with your pain,
but it made you strong.
It gave you faith.

Now I know you were saying goodbye
the last time that we met.
I wasn't aware at the time,
but you knew more than I.

Show me a seashell.
Put one in my path.
Make it sparkle
so I will know.

FOUR FLOORS DOWN

I was assisting a family on the sixth floor in the hospital, as their ninety year old mother died. Numerous family members had congregated near the elevator. As I walked into the elevator to leave, I heard the patient's son state, "The funeral will be on Friday."

A few seconds later on my ride down, the elevator opened its doors onto the second floor. The second floor is where Labor and Delivery are located. I then heard someone say, "He has Jimmy's chin."

One family was grieving on the sixth floor, while another joyous over a birth four floors down. Both families were celebrating a life and making plans. A perfect example of the cycle of life.

FOUR FLOORS DOWN

Family at the bedside
when she took her final breath.
Ninety years of active living
flowing to an end.

Final arrangements to be made
to celebrate her life.
Sadness permeates the air
with laughter seeping in.

Four floors down
another family gathers.
Welcoming a new baby
after nine months of waiting.
Excitement fills the air.
Plans are being made.

Passages moments apart.
A celebration of two lives.
One that has run its course,
while another is just begun.
        Four floors down.

TOO SLOW

I had been following Carol, age sixty-two, for over eighteen months. Carol was diagnosed with a brain tumor a few years prior to coming onto the hospice program. She had some confusion due to the cancer. On my first visit to their home, Carol and her daughter, Jennie, were loudly arguing. Both held their own in this dispute, which led me to believe that this was their typical communication style. A few months later, Jennie moved her mom into an Assisted Living Center. Jennie believed that her mom would live for only a few more months.

A year later, Carol was still alive, although slowly declining. Carol had become weaker and needed assistance with all of her activities. She spent most of her days sleeping, although she had a good appetite.

I always gave Jennie a telephone call when I made a visit to her mom. This poem was inspired after one of those telephone calls.

TOO SLOW

She has a lot of energy.
She keeps up a fast pace.
She stays constantly busy
or there's too much time to think.

She talks a mile a minute
interrupting as she goes.
She wants to tell you about her problems
and the progression that's too slow.

She and her mother don't get along.
It has always been that way.
Their conversations are full of anger,
criticism, reproach and blame.

Mom got cancer two years ago.
Things did not look good.
The doctors gave her about six months,
so she put mom in a home.

She visits mom once a week
for twenty minutes or so.
She flies in and then scurries out.
That is all the time she has.

Her days are packed and busy.
She has no time to waste.
So she'll tell those who will listen,
"She's dying way too slow."

A FINAL NUDGE

Being a medical social worker, I have participated in countless family meetings for the purpose of informing the family of the patient's medical status. Often serious decisions need to be made regarding treatment options. As a professional, one can be objective and compassionate to these families knowing the difficult decisions that need to be made.

Several years ago, my dad was on hospice for four days. We were blessed that he was able to be in an end-of-life facility. I felt familiar with all that was going on, but in addition I had the emotional turmoil that accompanies grief. It was such a surreal experience.

My dad was healthy for ninety-three of his ninety-four years. We had always talked about him coming to me at his death. We both assumed he would die peacefully in his sleep from old age as he had always been in good health.

My family and I were staying in a motel a few blocks from the hospice facility. I woke up from a sound sleep forty-five minutes after I went to bed. I got up and thought, "Dad, are you here?" Fifteen minutes later, hospice called to say that my dad died ten minutes before. They said that his breathing calmed five minutes before he died. I knew then that he did come to say goodbye. It gives me comfort to know that he was indeed on his way.

A FINAL NUDGE

He always promised to come to me
when it was his time to go.
To stop by to let me know
that he was on his way.

I always thought it would be quick.
A peaceful passing in his sleep.
I never dreamed it would be this way;
struggling at the end.

I awoke from a sound sleep
soon after I lay down.
My immediate thoughts were of him;
though not knowing it was his time.

Five minutes before he died
he came to say goodbye.
A final nudge to wake me up
to say he's on his way.

THE CALL

While my dad was on hospice, my family and I were staying in a motel close to the hospice facility. We all felt torn as we didn't want him to die, but then, we wanted it over. Even though it was only four days, somehow it felt that time just slowed down.

Each night before we went to bed, I would put my cell phone in the charger. I placed the charger across from our bed on the dresser. I will never forget that midnight call and seeing the red band of light flashing on my cell phone. That vision is etched in my mind forever.

THE CALL

We worried about the call.
Fearful each time the phone did ring.
Never knowing who it would be.

We dreaded the call.
Knowing it would eventually come
with the news we didn't want to hear.

We fretted,
we stressed.
The pressure profound.
How would we react
when the call did come?

Phone ringing at midnight.
This is the call.
Picking up the receiver
to hear the news
we knew we'd hear.

A sense of relief
    after
        The Call.

DO YOU KNOW?

I wrote this poem in memory of my dad. He was the one who helped me write my first poem when I was fourteen. He started writing poetry himself when he was in his eighties. At his memorial service, I read this poem as a tribute to him.

Having my dad on hospice for four days was a very surreal experience for me. As a social worker, I have been involved in so many similar situations, but as a daughter it comes from a totally different perspective. Being familiar with all the dynamics of hospice and grief, I was aware of the normalcy of what I was feeling, but I just didn't realize how deeply one could hurt. I have had other losses in my life, and fortunately one does forget the deep pain associated with each loss. Because I understood the process, I had expectations from myself to handle everything perfectly. I remember thinking at times that I thought I was stronger than I was. Fortunately, time does heal and the pain lessens if we are able to process our emotions in a way that works for us.

DO YOU KNOW?

Do you know
how much you influenced our lives?
    We know.

Do you know
you gave unconditional love?
    We know.

Do you know
you made us feel so special?
    We know.

Do you know
how hard it was to say goodbye?
    We know.

Do you know
how much you're missed?
    We know.

Do you know
you were so beautiful?
    We all know.
        We have always known.

SAM KNOWS

Part of the hospice social work role is to call families after the death for follow-up. This poem is what a daughter of a patient told me in one such bereavement call. Children grieve with the same emotions as adults. Toddlers show their grief in behavior. They do not have the vocabulary to express what they are feeling, but want to know what is going on. Quite often parents want to protect their children and keep them away from the situation. It is best to let the child guide you as to what they want to know. Describe to the child, at their age level, what is going on and ask them if they have any questions. Children will be honest with you.

The loss of a loved one allows a parent to teach their child tools to help deal with loss throughout their lifetime. Children will face multiple losses throughout their life. Not all loss is death. One feels grief when a best friend moves away or a parents' divorce.

I was counseling a five year old once whose Grandma was dying. I asked him if he had any questions. He replied, "If I ask it will make me sad." I told him that it was OK not to ask, but if he needed to ask, who would he ask? He said that he would ask his sister. It is best to allow the children the opportunity to ask those questions or say that it is OK to go play and have fun too.

Children can benefit from doing art to express what is inside them. Give a young child a blank piece of paper and some color crayons and tell them to draw a picture for their loved one. Their emotions will come out in their drawing.

SAM KNOWS

Sam has a special bond with his grandma.
A connection that only a one year old
and his grandma can share.
Nothing has changed since she's been sick.
She's still Grandma to Sam.

Grandma spends her days in bed now,
not eating or drinking at all.
She doesn't have much longer.
How much is Sam aware?

He's visiting with his family.
They'll stay another day or two.
Sam crawls around like usual
doing what one year olds just do.

They took a break from her bedroom
deciding to eat dinner as a group.
Sam joined his family in the kitchen
then took a beeline to Grandma's room.

He's never crawled to her room before.
They ran after him to check things out.
They found Sam staring at his grandma
observing her final breath.

How much did he understand?
Was his intuition all that strong?
Was he more connected than his family?
Only Sam and his grandma know.

MONEY VS. LOVE

I did a visit with a very troubled family. This family was extremely wealthy. According to the caregiver daughter Denise, mom gave money instead of love. Mom is dying from cancer and dementia. All the adult children tend to stay away except Denise, who herself suffers from a mental illness. Her coping skills are fragile and she is right on the edge.

On one particular visit, I found Denise upset because of several recent incidences involving her siblings. I sat with her for over an hour listening to her rant and rave. She felt she had no support from her family. Although there was plenty of funds, Denise said her sister, who has control over mom's finances, won't spend the money to hire attendant care.

After leaving this home, I went out to my next visit. This case also involved an elderly mother suffering from terminal cancer. Her daughters were delightful and were there for her and each other. The ambiance of their home embraced healthy communication, humor and love.

Two similar situations, two different families, two different dynamics. Both families need support from the hospice team, but it can often be difficult and frustrating working with families like Denise's as there is not much we can offer them. Family dynamics that have been present for decades, cannot be dramatically altared during the short period of time that hospice is involved. My hope is to assist families to move forward as they are able.

MONEY VS. LOVE

They have all the money in the world.
They can purchase whatever they want.
They have all that one could ever need
       except love.

Mom gave money instead of love.
The children liked it that way.
They never had to work for it.
They never learned to love.

Another family financially strapped
but somehow they got by.
They learned early how to love.
They easily passed it around.

Now each mother is dying.
Both families are thrown off track.
Trying to find stability.
Each grabbing to hold on.

One family never learned how to give.
Money now isn't enough.
Chaos and anger reign.
Childhood lessons not taught.

Another family rallies to stay steady.
They've been through tough times before.
Holding together onto the course.
Love is all that they need.

Two families in crisis.
Two journeys side by side.
One is fighting the rapids
while the other is gliding by.

ANOTHER NORMAL DAY

Maria was a forty-nine year old female who suffered from ALS (Lou Gehrig's Disease). She had an attendant caring for her during the day. Her husband, Jose, continued her care when he returned home from work each night. Maria was wheelchair bound and used a writing board to communicate. She needed help with all of her activities of daily living. The couple had two young daughters, Sophia, age nine, and Carmen, age six.

Jose died suddenly after a short bout with pneumonia. The family were told that he died from exhaustion. Maria's sister, Ann, moved the three of them in with her and her family. Ann lived two hours north of her sister's home. Ann immediately started guardianship paperwork for her two nieces.

Ann had two teenagers herself. Now there were seven people living in a small, three bedroom home. On my first visit to the home, I spent time with nine year old Sophia. She was pretty matter of fact about everything. In fact, she spoke openly with me about her dad dying while she played a video game. Sophia is nine going on instant maturity. This poem was triggered by my conversation with her.

ANOTHER NORMAL DAY

She is pretty good in school.
She gets decent grades.
She always does her homework
although math is just okay.

Her dad died suddenly four weeks ago.

She loves to play video games.
Coloring is still pretty cool.
She has a few special girlfriends,
although they now live far away.

She had to move to another town.

She loves to watch basketball.
She's pretty good at soccer too.
She can jump high on the trampoline.
She loves being outdoors.

Her mom is dying from ALS.

She is only
      nine years old.

ONE LAST REQUEST

Brenda, eighty years old, was dying from lung disease and had been hospitalized for several days because of complications. Her daughter, Janice, had been caring for her mother for several months. I found out later that Brenda also had three sons. They all lived out of state and had not spoken with their mother for several years.

Brenda had completed a will years ago, but wanted to update it leaving everything to Janice. She had requested my assistance in helping her with this. I picked up a Yellow Pages and attempted to call several attorneys without any success. Being a Saturday, I wasn't surprised. Two siblings were visiting their mother in the next bed and had overheard our conversation. They shared that they knew an attorney who could help us. I called the attorney and, over the telephone, he instructed me on the proper way to word the will.

I then typed up a copy for Brenda as he directed. I read the will to her and she quickly signed and dated it at the bottom of the page. Immediately the stress dissolved from Brenda's face into an image of total peace. She died several hours later.

A few months afterwards, all who were involved were subpoenaed. Brenda's three estranged children were contesting the will. I realized then that it hadn't been important to me if the will was legal, but that Brenda died believing it was. I felt she was able to die in peace because she believed her daughter Janice would be the sole beneficiary.

The case was settled out of court one day before it was scheduled to begin. I was never aware of the outcome of the settlement, but was grateful that I was able to honor Brenda's last request.

ONE LAST REQUEST

Her one last request,
hours before she died,
was to make a final will
bequeathing her assets
to her youngest daughter
who was standing vigil
at the bedside.

Her ashen face lined with worry,
stressing over the fact
that all was not complete.
One single task left to be done.
A final page to be written.

Formal words quickly typed
on a plain piece of white paper,
clearly instructing her wishes
after she was gone.

Witnessed by two strangers,
her signature triggers a
descending transformation
erasing decades of fatigue
from her weary face.
A face now aglow with peace
at the completion of her
one last request.

Months after her death,
attorneys tied up in court.
Siblings fighting siblings.
Rivalry, anger, conquest.
Assets now more important
that mom's
    one last request.

111

AMAZING GRACE

I had been following Ed, a wonderful sixty-four year old gentleman for several months. He was dying of cancer, but his strong faith and family helped him tremendously. Ed was the youngest of sixteen children and told of stories about the small town where he grew up. Ed said it was a "Poke and Plum" town. He said once you poked your head into town, you were plum out of it. He also shared that his town was so small that the entering sign was also the exiting sign.

I went out for a visit and it was obvious that Ed's time was near. Ed's entire family, with the exception of one daughter who was sleeping, were standing around his bed in the living room. An Elvis Presley CD was playing in the background. His wife, Suzanne, switched the music from Elvis to another CD as she said that Ed only liked Elvis's Gospel songs and not the ballads.

Five minutes later, his other daughter awoke and walked into the room. The moment she walked in, Ed took his last breath. All of a sudden, Elvis was singing "Amazing Grace". It seemed louder than the previous music. Suzanne had just switched off that CD to the next CD on the player. I had a hunch that Ed may have switched back to Elvis's "Amazing Grace" to propel him on his way.

AMAZING GRACE

He had an amazing faith.
He knew he'd be just fine,
but he worried about his family
and those he'd leave behind.

These last few weeks were hard
as he slowly slipped away.
Though the presence of his family,
strong faith and Gospel music
kept him in a peaceful state of mind.

They knew his time was near
so the family stayed close-by.
With his Gospel music in the background,
we talked about his life.

He took his final breath
as his daughter walked into the room.
With his family standing by his side,
he knew then
        it was his time
                to let go.

Suddenly Elvis was singing "Amazing Grace".
We knew then
        that he chose that tune.

SEVENTY-TWO YEARS

There is something special about couples who hit milestones of fifty-plus years of marriage. Harry and Alice, both in their nineties, still showed affection toward each other that was there, I'm sure, from the beginning. Their family and friends only knew their life as a couple. Where there was one, there was the other. This couple truly exemplified "The Golden Years."

SEVENTY-TWO YEARS

Seventy-two years.
What was it like to be married that long?
Most of us will probably never know.

A lifetime of love,
a treasure trove of memories,
millions of stories
too numerous to remember.

Just when we thought
it would last forever;
it quietly ended
just before noon today.

After so many years of living
he could go no further.
His body just wore out
with her laying naturally by his side,
just like she has done
for seventy-two years.

A FEW MINUTES

Bob, seventy-one, had just been on hospice one day. Bob and his wife, Theresa, had recently been told by his Oncologist that he had only a few weeks left to live. The family hoped Bob would outlive the doctor's poor prognosis.

Theresa made an urgent call to hospice requesting that someone come out right away. She noticed that Bob's breathing was erratic and shallow. She didn't know what to do. When I knocked on the front door, Bob's sister-in-law Gladys, quickly told me that the doctor said he would live for several weeks.

I walked into the home finding Theresa sitting at the bedside. I immediately recognized that Bob was actively dying. Before I said anything, Theresa asked me if he was dying. I told her yes. A few minutes later, Bob peacefully died with both of us at his side.

It is an honor to be in a home when someone dies. I see it as a gift when allowed to witness a patient's last breath. It is amazing to me as one moment they are on this earth and the next moment they are in another dimension. I always want to know what the patient is experiencing and is it as wonderful as we hope it will be.

A FEW MINUTES

I got there right on time
with a few minutes to spare.
Promising to come within the hour,
I showed up promptly at their door.

They directed me to the room
where his wife was at his side,
wondering if his time was near.
Needing so much to know.

His breathing was erratic.
A deep breath now and then.
One final gasp
a few minutes
after I walked in.

Being a stranger in his home
I didn't expect to receive
such a profound, intimate gift,
etched forever in my mind.

Lasting only
a few minutes
of his time.

THREE WORDS

I was asked by our Hospice Volunteer Coordinator to teach a three hour volunteer training class on "The Psycho-Social Impact of Dying". The class was attended by twenty hospice volunteer candidates.

I started off the class by sharing how I got into Hospice. I then asked the students to each share the story of their journey to Hospice. Brad, one of the students, was sitting in the last row on the end. He was the last to speak and shared that I was the reason that he was there. Brad said that I was the social worker when his mother was on hospice. I felt bad not remembering his mother or him, but he said that his mother died ten months ago and I had only visited twice. He said that she was on hospice for only two weeks.

It brought to mind how we all touch each others lives. It is easy to recognize when someone touches us, but one does not easily see our own impact on others. I felt so honored as I made a difference to him. I know too that Brad made a tremendous difference to me. It continually flows both ways. Thank you Brad.

THREE WORDS

I don't remember saying it,
but he will never forget.
Words etched forever in his mind.
A comfort while his mother lay dying.

He said I only visited twice
as her decline was swift.
I felt bad not remembering him,
but he didn't mind at all
as it's been almost a year.

He said he'll never forget me
and the comfort that he felt
when we walked into her room
and I said those three words.

Neither could predict
the impact of that day
as I gently touched her foot
and turned to him and said,
"She looks peaceful."

He may not remember saying it,
but I will never forget.
Three words etched forever in my mind,
"I'll always remember."

CONTROL

This poem is about a very focused seventy-five year old who was dying from pancreatic cancer. John had been married for sixteen years to his present wife Anne. Anne had three adult children from a previous marriage. John was an only child and had no children of his own. No one ever demanded anything from him.

Anne said that he had become verbally abusive in the past few years. She believed things changed when he was diagnosed with cancer. My sense of it all was that John probably always had been a bit selfish and self-centered whereby his behavior only escalated after the diagnosis.

This couple shared a beautiful home on five acres with a tremendous view. The home was decorated perfectly, although I felt no warmth there. When I asked Anne how she was coping, John seemed surprised that she felt anything at all. After all, he stated, this was all about him. It was obvious that he had no sense of the feelings of those around him.

CONTROL

He has no brothers or sisters.
He grew up being alone.
The toys he wanted to play with
were always waiting there.
>He had total control.

Hard work has reaped him tremendous wealth.
His goals being simple and few.
Take what you need as you see it.
Turn it into a success.
>Take control.

His house reflects a prosperous career;
possessions of value and worth.
Tasteful artifacts proudly displayed.
All the comforts of home.

Cancer is now controlling his life.
He doesn't like it at all.
He lashes out to his wife
unaware of the impact on her.
Trying to keep control.

When asked about his life though,
he says it has been good.
He's done what he has wanted to do.
"I got my money's worth."

WAITING AROUND

It is not unusual for a patient to outlive their prognosis. Many are psychologically ready to die and yet it isn't happening quite as quickly as they thought it would. At one point, I had quite a few patients who were ready to die. They shared that they were just waiting for it to happen. I have often heard patients state that they feel like they are in Limbo. Typically during this time, they are totally dependant with not much of a quality of life for them. They say that they just want it over.

WAITING AROUND

I am just hanging out.
I have no goals,
I have no future.
Nothing to plan.
Just waiting around.

I wish it were over.
They told me it would be soon.
But time has come and gone
and I am just waiting around.

It's like I am in Limbo.
Nothing to do but sit here;
to remain,
        to linger,
                to hang out.

I'm just waiting around.

ONE HOUR

Lily, sixty-four, was dying of cancer after being diagnosed just two months prior. Lily's daughter, Marisa, asked me to write a letter verifying her mother's critical condition. Lily had family living in Peru. The plan was to get emergency Visas in order for the family to get to the United States to see Lily before she died.

About a week later, I called Marisa after learning that her mom had died over the previous weekend. Marisa said that her relatives arrived one hour after her mother had died.

Most often an hour passes by most of us without much notice. It typically doesn't seem like a great deal of time. In this case, one hour made all the difference.

ONE HOUR

It took about one hour
to write the letters she asked.
Sixty minutes of my time.
Not much at all.

Her aunt held onto the letters
as she was driven to the airport.
One hour until the flight to Peru.
Not much wait at all.

Multiple visits to the embassy.
The letters authenticating urgency.
Five days to issue emergency Visas.
Each hour blending into the next.

Flying family to the US.
Rushing to the bedside.

One hour
        too late.

CONVINCE ME

I followed Katherine, a seventy-five year old female, for six months. She suffered from lung cancer and had smoked cigarettes for years. She also liked her alcohol and didn't give up either habit until the last week of her life. Her daughter, Laura, was her caretaker. Laura was a recovering alcoholic and had been sober for over ten years.

Katherine had been doing pretty well until a fall confined her to her bed. I went out to visit five days after her fall. When I saw Katherine I was really shocked. She looked so much worse than when I last saw her two weeks before. She didn't seem to be aware that I was there as her eyes couldn't track me. Katherine was non-verbal and looked near death.

Laura and I went out to the kitchen to talk about the dying process. I shared that when it was all over, she would look back and realize that her mom had done it her way after all. She confided that she believed her mom was holding out for her and had concerns of her drinking again. I gave Laura tips on how to reassure her mom of her plan if she felt like she wanted a drink. Laura had already given her mom permission to go and was willing to also tell her mother her plan to contact her AA sponsor if she felt like she wanted to drink again.

At one point I heard someone saying "Hey", although it was soft and I wasn't sure if Katherine was calling for her daughter. It sounded like it came from the hallway. I looked at Laura who didn't pause in her conversation and so I just dismissed it as nothing.

A little while later I picked up my paperwork and was getting ready to leave. I had planned on leaving without saying goodbye to Katherine as I didn't want to disturb her. Katherine had been so confused when I initially went in and I didn't want to confuse her further. For some reason, I just stopped, put my papers down and went in to say goodbye anyway. When I went in, I found Katherine had died. I was able to console Laura and I believed Katherine left at that particular time knowing that Laura wouldn't be alone.

Later Laura brought up the sound she heard and we both became aware that it was the same sound that I heard. We both believed her mother came to the kitchen and heard us discussing Laura's plan. We were convinced that it was then that Katherine felt she could leave. Laura then knew that her mom did indeed die her own way.

CONVINCE ME

You can convince me about a lot of things.
That maybe someday we'll all get along;
that dogs will always remain man's best friend;
that cigarettes do cause lung cancer.

Other things, it wouldn't be so easy.
No debate is that compelling
as I need no further proof.
Some beliefs remain steadfast
and my truth shall remain strong.

You can never convince me
that she didn't know I was there
sitting at the kitchen table
giving support to her daughter.

You can never convince me
that we didn't hear her voice;
that she didn't say goodbye;
that we didn't witness her farewell.

I will always believe
that she knew I was there
so her daughter wouldn't be alone
when she chose to leave this earth.

I feel honored to have been there
but not really surprised at all.
She died the way she lived
doing things her way;
showing us after all
that she would always be a mom
especially at the end.

BE A MAN

I went out to do an initial visit on a new referral. The case involved sixty-four year old Evie, who suffered from breast cancer. While I was at the home, Evie received a phone call from her mother Rose. Rose told her daughter that she herself was just diagnosed with terminal cancer and would also be going onto hospice. Evie told me that her mother had struggled with Evie's terminal condition from the beginning. She felt that this was her mother's way of dying first, in order to avoid dealing with her own daughter's death. Within one month Rose did die from her disease. Evie followed in death two months later.

Evie's son, Jeff, witnessed his grandfather's struggle and told us that while Rose was dying, his grandfather, Jack, stood silently in the bedroom doorway shaking. It was then, that Jack curled up in the bed beside his wife of sixty-two years.

When men grieve, they often want to fix things as that is what they do well. They are not comfortable talking about their emotions as they have a fear of losing control Our society has dictated to men from Jack's generation that crying is a weakness. Men are more comfortable doing what they know. They may go work out in the yard, go jogging, or tinker with their car. Jack could not fix his wife's dying, but he could fix other things that would help him process his grief.

BE A MAN

He is from the old school
where you learned early to stay in control.
Don't ever cry, just hold it all in,
keep a stiff upper lip.
      Be a man.

He's done just that
for almost ninety years.
It must be working for him
as his wife has stood faithfully by his side
for more than sixty of those years.

He's helped raise his two daughters
who are attentive and love him a lot,
but he just goes quietly along his way
knowing it's important
      to be a man.

His wife became ill quite suddenly.
He knew she didn't have long,
so he curled up in bed beside her
hugging her and holding on tight.

She had to feel his love surround her
as she drifted from one world to the next.
Knowing what she had always known
that he would always and forevermore
      be her man.

THANK YOU

This poem was inspired after a visit with Rose and her family. Rose, sixty-six years old, suffered from terminal cancer. She was unconscious during my visit and had not eaten for several days. While being surrounded by her loved ones, it was obvious to the family that Rose would die soon. The family members were actively grieving and allowed me to guide them through this difficult time.

I was deeply touched by this family because of their outward display of affection toward their mother. While this family was my inspiration for this particular poem, I realized after completing it, that this poem could have been written about any hospice patient or family. With that in mind, I dedicate this poem to all hospice patients and their loved ones.

THANK YOU

Thank you for welcoming me into your home.
For making me feel so comfortable.
For sharing your personal thoughts,
      your deepest pain,
            your fears.

Thank you for allowing me into
the inner sanctum of your home.
For exposing your vulnerability
by discussing what is so difficult.
Letting me help you say goodbye.

You thank me for coming to visit
to help you through your pain.
You tell me I've made a difference
by your hugs,
      by your tears,
            by your words.

But it is you
who have made a difference
in my life and each of my days.
Trusting to share
the intimacy of dying
while accepting me into your world.

So I thank you.
Even though these words don't quite express
the depth of my soul,
      the gratitude in my heart,
            the indebtiness of my being.

These are the only words I know
to best express my appreciation towards you.
Two simple words that are really profound.
So from my heart and from my soul,
I simply say
      Thank you.

The rest is in God's hands.

11838419R0008

Made in the USA
Lexington, KY
04 November 2011